AF614921

by Nathan Sommer

Minneapolis, Minnesota

Credits

Cover, © L De Bruin/peopleimages.com/Adobe Stock; 4, © SolStock/iStock; 4–5, © South_agency/iStock; 6, © Real World People/Alamy Stock Photo; 7, © Greg Vaughn/Alamy Stock Photo; 8, © Helmut Corneli/Alamy Stock Photo; 8–9, © Travelscape Images/Alamy Stock Photo; 10, © WUT789/iStock; 11, © PeopleImages/iStock; 12, © schfer/iStock; 13, © Andrew Findlay/Alamy Stock Photo; 14, © Justine Evans/Alamy Stock Photo; 15, © ARCTIC IMAGES/Alamy Stock Photo; 16, © Dmytro Kosmenko/iStock; 17, © Westend61 GmbH/Alamy Stock Photo; 18, © Josie Elias/Alamy Stock Photo; 19, © Jeffrey Isaac Greenberg 3+/Alamy Stock Photo; 20, © ciud/iStock; 20–21, © Peter Gedei/Alamy Stock Photo; 22, © Ryan McGinnis/Alamy Stock Photo; 23, © Ryan McGinnis/Alamy Stock Photo; 24, © USGS/Wikimedia Commons; 24–25, © Bradley White/Alamy Stock Photo; 26, © Michael Williams/Alamy Stock Photo; 26–27, © AP/AP Newsroom; 28TL, © miodrag ignjatovic/iStock; 28TR, © Adrian Sherratt/Alamy Stock Photo; 28BL, © Justine Evans/Alamy Stock Photo; 28BR, © AzmanL/iStock; 29, © NurPhoto / Contributor/Getty Images; 31, © mbbirdy/iStock.

Bearport Publishing Company Product Development Team

Publisher: Jen Jenson; Director of Product Development: Spencer Brinker; Managing Editor: Allison Juda; Editor: Cole Nelson; Associate Editor: Naomi Reich; Associate Editor: Tiana Tran; Art Director: Colin O'Dea; Designer: Kim Jones; Designer: Kayla Eggert; Product Development Specialist: Owen Hamlin

Statement on Usage of Generative Artificial Intelligence

Bearport Publishing remains committed to publishing high-quality nonfiction books. Therefore, we restrict the use of generative AI to ensure accuracy of all text and visual components pertaining to a book's subject. See BearportPublishing.com for details.

Library of Congress Cataloging-in-Publication Data is available at www.loc.gov or upon request from the publisher.

ISBN: 979-8-89232-649-0 (hardcover)
ISBN: 979-8-89232-682-7 (ebook)

For more information, write to Bearport Publishing, 5357 Penn Avenue South, Minneapolis, MN 55419.

CONTENTS

EMPLOYED BY NATURE

From sandy coastlines and sparkling seas to lush forests and snow-capped mountains, there is so much beauty to be found in nature. Millions of people worldwide have turned their love for the outdoors into careers. And with such a huge world, it's no wonder these workers often face some of the most extreme conditions to get the job done. Are you ready to explore the wild world of nature careers?

Those who choose careers in nature may explore uncharted territories, conduct groundbreaking research, or even provide aid during disasters.

REACHING THE UNREACHABLE

Bush Pilot

Bush pilots operate small planes to fly people and goods to and from some of Earth's most remote places. Often, they don't have good maps and must rely on their skills and knowledge to safely navigate to uncharted regions of nature. These pilots fly planes equipped with floats, skis, and special tires that allow them to land on rocky mountaintops, upon icy glaciers, and on water.

What It Takes

- ☑ A pilot's license
- ☑ Aircraft safety and repair knowledge
- ☑ Navigation skills
- ☑ Wilderness survival skills
- ☑ A sense of adventure

Bush pilots must be able to repair their own airplanes while in remote locations.

Bush pilots sometimes land their planes on rivers, lakes, and oceans.

Bush pilots may be hired to fly conservationists around to help the scientists count wildlife populations.

JUMPING INTO THE DEEP

Commercial Diver

Commercial divers plunge below the waves to do many different jobs. Some divers help scientists research and protect underwater **environments**. The divers do this by collecting samples of rocks and kelp forests. Sometimes, they perform cleanup missions to remove garbage and **debris** from the ocean floor. Commercial divers can also do underwater repairs. They use electric tools to fix oil rigs in the ocean.

What It Takes

- ☑ Scuba certification
- ☑ Physical fitness
- ☑ Excellent swimming skills
- ☑ An ability to multitask
- ☑ Focus under pressure

Commercial divers often wear headlamps or carry other lights to see underwater.

Commercial divers often use scuba gear to breathe underwater.

Commercial divers can face the risks of **hypothermia**, drowning, electrocution, or even attacks from underwater creatures.

KEEPING EARTH SAFE

Conservationist

Conservationists are scientists whose main goal is to protect Earth's natural environments. These experts check plants, soil, and water for signs of disease, pollution, and **invasive species**. Some study the effects of human activities that cause **climate change** and how to best combat them. Additionally, conservationists work to educate the public about the importance of preserving Earth's resources. They spread the word to inspire people to take action on behalf of nature.

What It Takes

- ☑ An environmental science degree
- ☑ Good organization
- ☑ Great communication
- ☑ An ability to work with others
- ☑ A passion for protecting Earth

Some conservationists collect and study samples in nature to learn how environments are changing.

Conservationists help farmers plan how to best use their land while keeping the environment safe.

Some conservationists monitor wildlife. They track the health and strength of **endangered species** populations.

CATASTROPHE CLEANUP

Disaster Relief Worker

When natural disasters strike, who's there to help? Disaster relief workers head to the scenes of hurricanes, tornadoes, earthquakes, and tsunamis to aid victims. They often work in unpredictable weather to coordinate the evacuation of residents. They also provide medical care, food, water, and shelter to those affected by the disasters. Once storms have passed, these workers help the affected communities rebuild and prepare for possible future natural disasters.

What It Takes

- ☑ An emergency management degree
- ☑ Natural disaster knowledge
- ☑ A desire to help others
- ☑ Quick thinking
- ☑ Relationship-building skills
- ☑ An ability to work long hours

Disaster relief workers teach people how to make emergency preparedness kits.

Relief workers respond to many kinds of natural disasters, but floods are the most common.

Disaster relief workers often travel in boats through flooded areas.

ICE INVESTIGATOR

Glaciologist

Glaciologists are used to the cold! These scientists work in frozen conditions to study Earth's ice and how it's affected by climate change. To do this, glaciologists use **motion trackers** and **time-lapse cameras** to record the long-term movement of glaciers. They also collect samples of older ice to identify weather patterns from Earth's past. To gather these samples, glaciologists may use large drills or even don harnesses and lower themselves into the cracks of giant glaciers. *Brr!*

What It Takes

- ☑ An environmental science degree
- ☑ Tech skills
- ☑ An openness to living in remote areas
- ☑ A tolerance to extreme cold
- ☑ A love of ice

Glaciologists attach steel spikes to the bottom of their boots to keep from slipping on the ice.

The samples glaciologists drill out of glaciers are called ice cores.

Some glaciologists work in Antarctica, where there are no restaurants, grocery stores, or even roads!

THE DEADLIEST CLIMB

Mount Everest Expedition Guide

Mount Everest is the tallest—and one of the deadliest—mountains in the world. Expedition guides are professionals who help climbers reach the peak safely. They clear paths up the mountain and attach ropes at the most difficult parts. They also carry supplies, including tents and bottles of oxygen. If one of their climbers becomes sick or injured, these guides make sure the traveler receives medical care and is safely led down the mountain.

What It Takes

- ✓ Climbing **expertise**
- ✓ Knowledge of Everest's geography
- ✓ Leadership skills
- ✓ An ability to provide first aid
- ✓ Strong lungs

It takes longer than a month to climb to Mount Everest's peak.

Mount Everest guides provide inspiration and motivation when climbing gets tough.

Guides who are from the Mount Everest area are called sherpas. They act as Everest guides most frequently.

PATROLLING TO PROTECT

Park Ranger

Throughout the United States, there are hundreds of awe-inspiring **national parks**. Park rangers work night and day to protect these natural spaces and their wildlife. They patrol the grounds to make sure the habitats and animals are healthy. Park rangers also make sure visitors are safe and following the laws. To do this, rangers educate people on the rules and wildlife of the parks. They sometimes even perform search and rescue missions for lost hikers.

What It Takes

- ✓ An **ecology** or forestry degree
- ✓ Public-safety training
- ✓ Knowledge of national park history
- ✓ Hiking experience
- ✓ Strong communication skills

Park rangers sometimes capture and treat injured or sick animals.

Park rangers patrol national parks on all-terrain vehicles, snowmobiles, boats, or horseback.

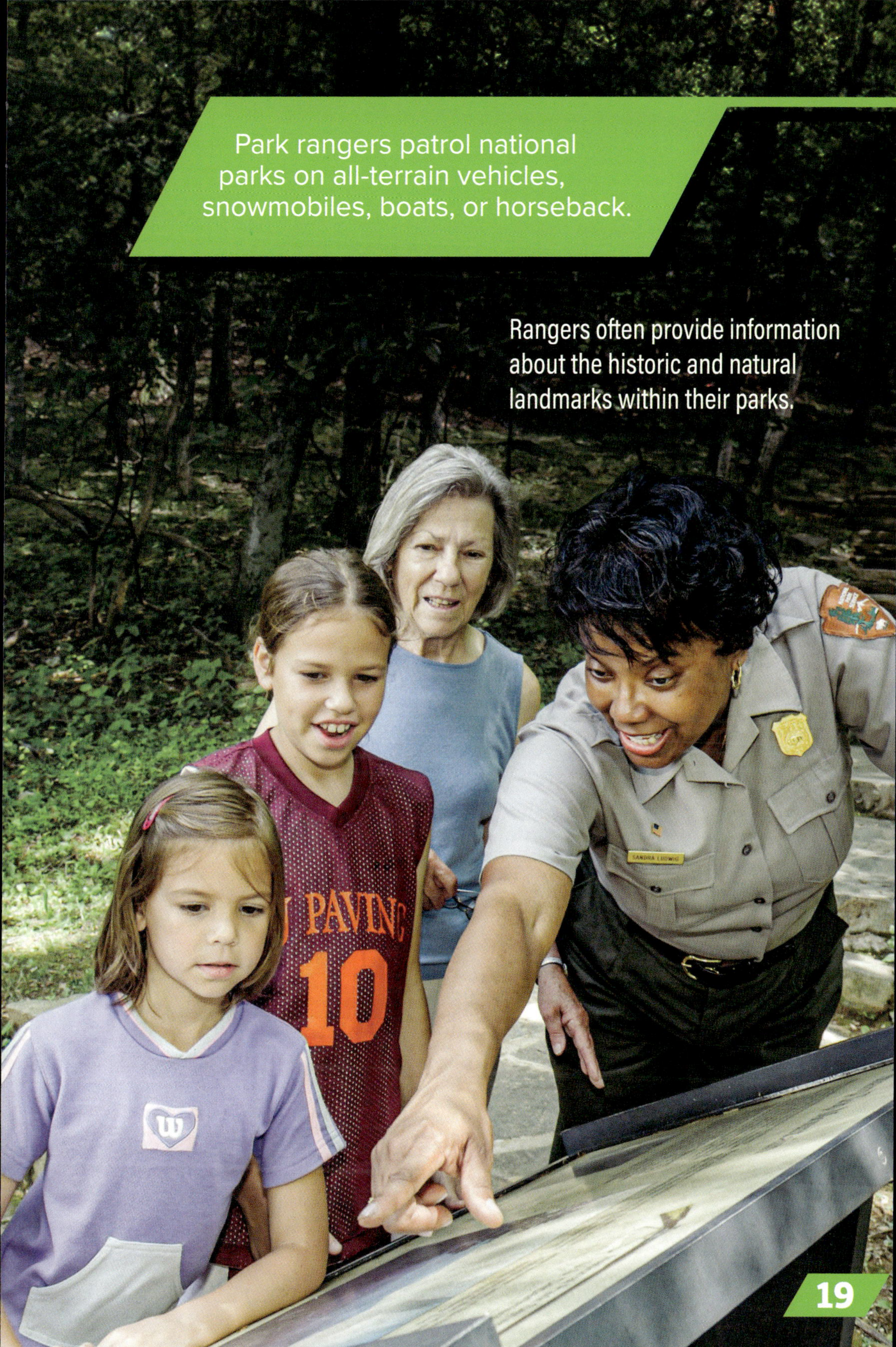

Rangers often provide information about the historic and natural landmarks within their parks.

EXPLORING THE UNKNOWN

Speleologist

Journeying into Earth's caverns is all in a day's work for speleologists! These scientists explore deep and dark caves to learn how the hollow chambers formed. They collect samples of rocks, organisms, and water to study life within the caves. However, the twisting paths and tight tunnels inside these natural landforms can often be dangerous. Speleologists spend a lot of time planning and mapping out the safest routes.

What It Takes

- ☑ An Earth science degree
- ☑ Cave exploration experience
- ☑ A willingness to work in tight spaces
- ☑ Being comfortable in the dark
- ☑ Navigation skills

Some speleologists study minerals, such as crystals, that form in caves.

Speleologists wear helmets, coveralls, and gloves when exploring caves.

To date, the deepest cave explored by speleologists reaches about 7,260 feet (2,210 m) underground!

INTO THE RAGING WEATHER

Storm Chaser

Most people hide from dangerous storms. Not storm chasers! These fearless professionals head toward tornadoes, hurricanes, and thunderstorms to study them in real time. They monitor wind speeds, temperatures, and **radar** images to locate bad weather. Once near—or even inside—a storm, they collect more data with cameras and special sensors. This information can be used to determine accurate forecasts to warn the public that dangerous weather may be heading their way.

What It Takes

- ☑ **Meteorology** experience
- ☑ Photography and video skills
- ☑ Radar and satellite imaging knowledge
- ☑ A calm head in stressful situations
- ☑ A commitment to safety

Storm chasers usually work in teams.

Storm chasers may spend days on the road while tracking a single storm.

Some chasers drop sensors into hurricanes from airplanes. Data from the sensors helps determine a hurricane's strength.

LAVA LOVER

Volcanologist

Volcanologists study what makes volcanoes tick! These scientists use tools, such as **seismographs**, to measure underground activity that helps them predict volcanic eruptions. They also collect rock, gas, and lava samples to study what is happening inside a volcano's **magma chambers**. When a volcano erupts, volcanologists use satellite images and **infrared cameras** to detect and track the activity from a safe distance.

What It Takes

- ☑ A **geology** degree
- ☑ Hiking and climbing experience
- ☑ Excellent research skills
- ☑ A love of travel

Volcanologists carefully cool samples of very hot lava in cans of water.

Special suits keep volcanologists safe while studying active volcanoes.

Volcanologists work with local governments to create evacuation plans for people living near active volcanoes.

WILDFIRE WARRIOR

Wildland Firefighter

Wildland firefighters stop nature's most destructive fires. Some of them work from helicopters equipped with giant buckets that can drop hundreds of gallons of water on a blaze. Others parachute from airplanes into hard-to-reach areas to face a fire directly. On the ground, wildland firefighters use chainsaws, shovels, and even controlled fires to remove plants that burn easily. This creates a path called a **firebreak**, which helps stop wildfires from spreading.

What It Takes

- ☑ Strength to handle heavy equipment
- ☑ High heat tolerance
- ☑ Teamwork skills
- ☑ Being unafraid of heights

Firefighting helicopters can carry up to 700 gallons (2,650 L) of water!

Wildland firefighters help stop about 70,000 wildfires in the United States each year.

Wildland firefighters are trained to provide first aid to wildfire survivors.

NATURE'S EXPERTS

It's safe to say Earth is a better place thanks to those employed in nature careers. People who take on these jobs may face tough conditions, but they often find their work fulfilling. With a little passion, knowledge, and determination, you could have a nature career, too!

NATURE CAREER SPOTLIGHT

Kami Rita

Kami Rita was the first person to have climbed Mount Everest 30 times. The Himalayan expedition guide first reached the peak in 1994. Almost every year since then, he has helped climbers safely reach the top of Mount Everest. His knowledge and experience make one of the world's deadliest climbs safer for countless adventurers.

GLOSSARY

climate change changes in Earth's usual weather patterns, including the warming of the air and oceans, due to human activities

debris pieces of things that have been damaged or destroyed

ecology the science related to the relationships between living things and their environments

endangered species animals or plants that are at risk of dying out completely

environments surroundings and conditions of natural areas

expertise specialty knowledge or skills on a subject

firebreak a path cleared around a forest fire to stop flames from spreading

geology the science that deals with Earth's rocks

hypothermia the condition of having a dangerously low body temperature

infrared cameras cameras that detect heat energy and process it as images

invasive species plants or animals that have been moved from their habitat into another habitat in which they do not naturally belong

magma chambers large pools of liquid rock beneath a volcano's surface

meteorology the science that deals with weather and weather forecasting

motion trackers devices that record movement

national parks areas of land set aside by the government to protect the animals and plants that live there

radar a device that uses radio waves to locate and track objects that are far away

seismographs instruments that detect earthquakes and measure their power

time-lapse cameras cameras that take photos regularly over long periods of time

READ MORE

Golkar, Golriz. *Ancient Ice: What Glaciers Reveal about Climate Change.* North Mankato, MN: Capstone Press, 2024.

Haynes, Danielle. *Scaling Mount Everest (Life on the Edge).* Buffalo, NY: PowerKids Press, 2024.

Walker, Tracy Sue. *Wildlife Conservation Technology (Saving Animals with Science).* Minneapolis: Lerner Publications, 2024.

LEARN MORE ONLINE

1. Go to **FactSurfer.com** or scan the QR code below.
2. Enter "**Nature Careers**" into the search box.
3. Click on the cover of this book to see a list of websites.

INDEX

ABOUT THE AUTHOR

Nathan Sommer graduated from the University of Minnesota with degrees in journalism and political science. He enjoys camping, hiking, and writing in his free time. He lives in Minneapolis, Minnesota.